Yellow Umbrella Books are published by Red Brick Learning
7825 Telegraph Road, Bloomington, Minnesota 55438
http://www.redbricklearning.com

Library of Congress Cataloging-in-Publication Data
Bauer, David (David S.)
    [My apple tree. Spanish & English]
    My apple tree/by David Bauer = Mi manzano/por David Bauer.
    p. cm.
    Summary: "Simple text and photos present the life cycle of an apple tree"— Provided
by publisher.
    Includes index.
    ISBN-13: 978-0-7368-6010-9 (hardcover)
    ISBN-10: 0-7368-6010-X (hardcover)
    1. Apples—Juvenile literature. I. Title: Mi manzano. II. Title.
SB363.B3818 2006
634'.11—dc22   2005025843

Written by David Bauer
Developed by Raindrop Publishing

Editorial Director: Mary Lindeen
Editor: Jennifer VanVoorst
Photo Researcher: Wanda Winch
Adapted Translations: Gloria Ramos
Spanish Language Consultants: Jesús Cervantes, Anita Constantino
Conversion Assistants: Jenny Marks, Laura Manthe

Photo Credits
Cover: David Frazier/Corbis; Title Page: New York Apple Association; Page 4: Gary
Sundermeyer/Capstone Press; Page 6: Gary Sundermeyer/Capstone Press; Page 8: Patrick
Johns/Corbis; Page 10: William Allen; Page 12: Mark E. Gibson/Corbis; Page 14: Mark
E. Gibson/Corbis; Page 16: Mark E. Gibson/Corbis

1 2 3 4 5 6 11 10 09 08 07 06

My Apple Tree
by David Bauer

Mi manzano
por David Bauer

Yellow
Umbrella
Books
for early readers

My apple tree
grows leaves.

Mi manzano
crece hojas.

My apple tree
grows flowers.

Mi manzano
crece flores.

My apple tree
grows apples.

Mi manzano
crece manzanas.

My apple tree
grows lots of apples!

Mi manzano
crece muchas manzanas.

We pick apples
from my apple tree.

Recogemos manzanas
de mi manzano.

We eat apples
from my apple tree.

Comemos manzanas
de mi manzano.

Leaves fall from my apple tree. Soon they will grow back again.

Este es mi manzano. Pronto va a tener manzanas.

Index

Índice